The Shape of Matter

Melissa Allgrim

BookLeaf
Publishing

India | USA | UK

Presentation by *BookLeaf Publishing*

Web: www.bookleafpub.com

E-mail: info@bookleafpub.com

ISBN: 9789363313828

First edition 2024

For my friends and companions without which none of this would be possible.

ACKNOWLEDGEMENT

This is for all of the people, places, and
experiences that helped me get here.

PREFACE

Thank you for taking the time to check out my book. If you like it, please share it.

Infinite

Infinite Abundance Supports You.

Shed distractions.

Embrace
All That You Are.

Self-Possession

you possess
you have
an amazing

amount of potential.

you are aware of
your potential and

you create your own,
love,

meaning, and motivation in a safe,
healthy, pure,
flexible,
supple,

whole connected vessel.

Very soon,
Sooner than we realize,

This Unbounded, Unending
Resilience will
Be known.

Agreements

Agreements
Assumptions
Culture

Context
Value Set
Awareness

In situations where responsibility is unclear,

all involved parties agree to resolve the matter in
good faith,
and with the least amount of damage,

physical and financial,

that will injure (see also: hurt)
all entities least;

whichever scenario in which we all agree.

Balance

Manage your Attitude.
Keep an eye on it.

By Striking the Balance, your ship will sail you
wherever You Wish to go.

Remember

I am allowed to feel happy without feeling guilty.
You are allowed to feel happy without feeling guilty.
We are allowed to feel happy without feeling guilty.

I am allowed to feel healthy without feeling guilty.
You are allowed to feel healthy without feeling guilty.
We are allowed to feel healthy without feeling guilty.

I am allowed to breathe without feeling guilty.
You are allowed to breathe without feeling guilty.
We are allowed to breathe happy without feeling guilty.

I am allowed to enjoy my life.
You are allowed to enjoy your life.
We are allowed to enjoy life.
Alone and Together.

I am allowed to heal fully.
You are allowed to heal fully.
We are allowed to heal fully.

I am allowed to enjoy this life.
You are allowed to enjoy this life.
We are allowed to enjoy this life.
Alone and Together.

Breathe.
I am allowed to Breathe.
You are allowed to Breathe.
We are allowed to Breathe.
Breathe without worry.
Breathe without doubt.
Breathe without guilt or fear.

Motivation

Motivation is
Your Craving

for continued
incremental

life-enhancing actions.

rest - hydration - movement.

you cannot beat yourself into better.
you can accept yourself there, though.

Motivation is
Your Craving

for continued
incremental

life-enhancing actions.

Keep creating life-enhancing action in your life.
Continue creating life-enhancing actions in your
life.

Cultivate creating life-enhancing actions in this life.

Gratitudinal

Pendulums Swinging
on
Ellipses.

The fact that I get to
Choose My Choices.

Read. Reflect. Respond. Rest.
Intent. Belief. Love. Desire.

Grace.
Authenticness.
Patience.
Integrity.
Self-care.
Motivation.

Love Remade Daily

Kindness
Compassion
Patience

Peace
Calm
Non-Attachment

Honest
Pure
True

Acceptance and Appreciation
Let Gravity Guide You

Angel

It became apparent
Upon their first interaction

With an entity from Earth
That it would be

In their own best interests

To remove their wings
Before engaging with
Another.

Lead

Create Space
Lead

Relax

Stress Deduction
Creates Stress Reduction

Eustress is success in disguise;
Seeing what is on its way.

Never

Never doesn't really exist.
Never is merely a way we try to understand
things.

A way to share advice,
A way to dispel worry.

Never push into your puddle.
She never allowed herself to be clouded.

By saying,
By thinking,
that Nothing is,
We convince ourselves to allow less.

Live your dream and people will buy it.

Saiqe

Temerity could result in Sequela.

Space

15

Space: a word of curse to be used when, if ever, you sense being constricted to open things up through grace, a gentle response, a creative revolution.

Sage

as a sage
i am an ova
the beginnings of a map.

we each have three heart bowls.

in each is a new armor,
and in each are a different gym,

each able to speak at the three
different kneads

you have
you are
you want

Happy

Healthy Active Positive Productive You

Helpful Appreciative Patient Peaceful You

Honest Able Persistent Present You

Honorable Accountable Prepared Pleasant You

Solstice

Today feels like one of those
Days when you can really

Feel the tilt
of the Planet.

For the Birds

Oh, melodious warblers,
chippers, chirpers,
trillers and caw-ers,

Your flight
invites
wonderous respect.

To those that sing
Without worry
of an audience,

Those who worry not
about bough breakage.

Pivot

The ability to pivot.
The ability to accept things as they are.
The ability to let go.
The ability to forgive myself, fully.
The ability to forgive others unconditionally.

Emotions

All emotions
are

Your perception of Freedom
and
Your perception of Bondage.

Emotion is
Your Perception of
Freedom in a complete connection with who you
really are,

Emotion is
Your Perception of
Bondage from the severe pinching yourself off
from who you really are.

Emotion is each moment
Choosing
Balancing

Which one do you want and
Which one you need
To be more

Regeneration

22

Healthy Organs
Healthy Bones
Balanced Healing
Calming Tones

Inbetween

Perceptive
Intuitive
Logical

Contented
Happy
Safe
Supported

I am the pattern
I am comfort
I am held

I feel the pattern
I feel comfort
I feel held

I choose the be a part of the pattern
I choose to be comforted
I choose to be held

I love
I speak
I see
I know